If I Die Before

I Wake

G.H. Cline

"The enemy continues to hope that America's will to persevere can be broken. Well, he is wrong. America will persevere. Our patience and our perseverance will match our power. Aggression will never prevail."

Lyndon Baines Johnson

State of the Union ~ 17 January 1968

Dedicated To:

All of the Soldiers that died early that morning on L.Z. Peanuts,
May 4, 1968:

The over 58,000 men and women that perished throughout the
Vietnam Conflict and the approximated 900,000 to 2,000,000
Vietnamese casualties of this war.

1 November 1955 to 30 April of 1975

"The Inhumanity of War"

Note: November 11,1961 President John Kennedy decided to commit
U.S. advisers to South Vietnam in excess of the number permitted in the
Geneva Accords of 1954.

Acknowledgment

The Study Of Vietnam :

 by George C. Herring

In Retrospect / The Tragedy and lessons of Vietnam:

 by Robert S. McNamara

Dereliction Of Duty:

 Lyndon Johnson, Robert McNamara, The Joint Chiefs of Staff, and the lies that led to Vietnam:

 by H. R. Mc Master

Dispatches:

 by Michael Herr

The Wise Minority:

 An Argument for Draft Resistance and Civil Disobedience

 by Leon Friedman

With Special Thanks to:

Blue Mount Publishers and specifically James Duran and Hazel Brian, including their multi-faceted Team of diligent and creative professionals.

Ed Salven for his generous proficiency in this manuscripts review.

And With Supreme Thanks to **Windsor Betts** for her meticulous editing skills.

. . . The year was 1968. I had already been in Vietnam for five months. I was 20 years old.

"Ours is not to reason why. Ours is but to do or die."

This strange and questionable Army slogan swirled within our minds like haunting whispers that occur in nightmares. Who knew that the First Air Cavalry Division could loan our Battalion to the Marines, much less why! Even more than the Cav., the Marines liked to keep their noses in the shit, staying where the action was. Except this time there was just too much action; too much enemy artillery fire out of Cambodia, and too many armored tanks on loan from Communist China crawling over this northernmost part of Southeast Asia. The President knew all of this, along with the Joint Chiefs of Staff, but as far as the American public knew, none of it existed.

Our Battalion, the 1/77th Artillery, as well as Infantry platoons A/1/5, and in fact, most of the combat soldiers in Vietnam, had already heard the horror stories about the Marines being all but wiped out at Khe Sanh. So when the orders came down for us to once again 'pack-up' and 'move-out' to this same deadly vicinity, we shrugged, took a deep breath, and began throwing our personal belongings into our duffel bags. The Gun Personnel were stacking their ammo into net-slings, readying the Howitzers for the move; as we continued breaking down the Fire Direction Control, packing the charts and maps, wrapping up the communication radios, the generator batteries, the antennas and everything we needed to run the FDC, the brains behind our Artillery Battery, were again loaded and stuffed into various containers and placed in or tied onto the

Captain's Jeep for transport.

But this time it was different. An awkward stillness fell over our Battery as we prepared for departure. An unknown silence that seemed to be part of our collective consciousness preoccupied the entire *Landing Zone* (LZ), as though some primordial fear had reached out from its eerie depths and draped over us like a fog. The Infantry didn't seem to notice. They seldom noticed subtleties unless it was some sixth sense as to where Charley might hit next. Besides, they were busy grabbing their few belongings and preparing to jump aboard the next awaiting Huey-Gunship - 'Gung-Ho' ready to hit another LZ and kick-ass, head out into the field to pull another reconnaissance mission. They were the first to lift off and maneuver into a formation awaiting the rest of us.

Our Bird Colonel, Birth Control 6, was already observing this move from his Loach helicopter at a higher, more protected elevation while the last of our Chinook's arrived and hovered overhead. Sand, dirt, and dust swirled everywhere with the force of a small tornado as we tried to pass the thick nylon sling under the jeep's chassis and around its sides; pulling the large steel rings up to where the hovering chopper swayed rhythmically just above our heads. We were being pushed around by gale force winds from the rotors like buoys adrift in a troubled sea. But finally, while constantly wiping the stinging grit from our eyes, we snagged the hook beneath the chopper's belly and the Chinook lifted off taking away the jeep with all our belongings beneath its belly. The rest of the FDC personnel, our Captain, and I now found the last awaiting Huey. We jumped aboard and lifted off to follow the Chinooks with our jeep and the 105 Howitzers swaying gently beneath them. Pulling away, we all looked back one last time and said a silent goodbye to that stinking garbage dump of an LZ. It was simply another temporary home now abandoned, left for the rats.

Having the Captain aboard, our chopper caught up with and passed the Infantry Gun Ships to take the lead of the Landing Party as we caravanned through the mid-day Vietnamese sky. I was sitting next to the door gunner for the M-60 machine gun and was able to look out over the horizon. Here I was taken again by the beauty this country must once have had; long before the numerous wars blew gaping holes into her pristine resort-quality complexion. I had heard that even between the wars there were times when great hunting resorts spotted the landscape and the movie stars of yesteryear with dignitaries and diplomats would all come to bag their 'Big Game' of choice, to then trophy their cherry wood paneled smoking room walls back home. They would sit comfortably on screened verandas watching the spectacular sunsets and sip vintage Port, smoke Cuban cigars, and tell their hunting adventures of the day. But the "Big Game hunting" and "Vietnam Vacation Resorts" had passed away all too quickly. And now we sat, vibrating across its sky in an open-sided helicopter in the middle of yet another war. I checked my watch and realized that an hour had already passed and this was, by far, our longest move yet.

We usually didn't know much about our next move, but this time, becoming attached to the Marines, with all of the Khe Sanh rumors was an unwanted exception. We were most certainly heading North, and North was not the place to be heading in Vietnam.

I turned to look between the pilot and co-pilot, out the front windscreen of the chopper as we finally began our descent towards a little finger of a knoll that jutted from the side of a larger flatter area of a then continuing mountain range. It was a virgin LZ and once we were dropped off we would have to dig in and build all of our personal hooches, ammo dumps, FDC bunker, et cetera, et cetera. I just couldn't figure out which was worse: to land in another stinking shit-hole of a deserted LZ, or have to break your ass digging in, filling and stacking sandbags to construct your own.

"Look, you can see Laos," the co-pilot yelled over the loud rotor roar of the engine pointing to his left. I looked across to the mountainous range on the horizon as our chopper continued its decent. Suddenly, the pilot screamed something and banked hard left, almost throwing me into the back of the door gunner. "It's Hot! The LZ is hot!" the pilot yelled. "We're taking small arms fire!" While the pilot fought the controls the co-pilot grabbed for the radio transmitter and reported the event to the following Chinooks and the Infantry Gunships. Our chopper pilot and co-pilot's heads bobbed and weaved as they put us into a tight 45 degree bank, with the co-pilot still transmitting to Birth Control 6, who was following high above. We all held tight as our entire Battery and Infantry landing party turned for safety, lifting back up to gain altitude and circle our targeted Landing Zone.

The small arms fire could have come from anywhere in these high perched, canopy covered mountains, and the arrogance of small arms against a full-scale Artillery and Infantry landing party just proved the enemy's self-assured pride. They were just sending us a little love letter letting us know that they were at home, *and would be waiting.*

*   *   *

"You have a row of dominoes set up; you knock over the first one, and what will happen to the last one is that it will go over very quickly."

Dwight D. Eisenhower, 1954

The Republic of Vietnam was divided into four corps tactical zones, each of which was a political as well as military jurisdiction. I Corps bordered the Demilitarized Zone (DMZ), which separated

South Vietnam from its northern enemy and, in fact, was far from demilitarized. On the west, I Corps abutted Laos and the enemy bases supplied by the Ho Chi Minh Trail. North Vietnamese Army (NVA) troops could easily invade the region from either direction, and their long-range artillery could shell the northern Quang Tri Province from the relative safety of North Vietnam and Laos. I Corps covered 10,000 square miles. This was Charley's country; the same mountainous jungle terrain where in the summer of 1967 the maddening Battle of Dak To finally ended at the top of Hill 875. The U.S. announced that 4,000 of the enemy had been killed; it had been the purest of slaughters. Our losses were bad, but it was clearly another 'American Victory.' But when the top of the hill was reached, the number of Charley or NVA found was four (4). Of course, more died, hundreds more, but the corpses kicked, counted, photographed, and buried numbered only four. The truth was we killed a lot of Communists, but that was all we did because the number of Communist dead meant nothing, changed nothing.

Everything up in this part of the Vietnam Mountains was weird and unearthly, and would be that way even if there was no war. We were in a place where we didn't belong, a place where they didn't play with mystery but killed you straight off just for trespassing. Even the names of the towns sent chills running deep into your marrow: Kontum, Dak Mot Lop, Buon Blech, Pleiku, Plei Me, Plei Vidrin. Just moving through those towns or being based somewhere above them spaced you out in some unknown way.

I wished I was stoned and spaced out sitting in my hooch on some large safe Base Camp listening to music on my cassette instead of caught up in the reality of our chopper and Landing Party taking enemy fire. Our co-pilot and Birth Control 6 had been in continuous communication when finally, the Pilot gave the co-pilot another hand signal, then yelled back and forth to each other, to finally turn and yell to us, "We're going to move out of the quadrant while they shell below." Again, we tried to decipher the information over the loud roar of the chopper rotors, but we understood what was happening. Our Captain seemed calm, holding on with the rest of us, cramped into the belly of this rattling and shaking gun-ship, now high over the mountainous jungles. I reckoned a Captain was supposed to look calm during such situations to project confidence. But I wasn't sure that it was working. I for one was scared shitless.

Birth Control 6 had called-in for a large 155 Howitzer artillery barrage to spread over the entire grid below, crisscrossing around our targeted Landing Zone. "That should teach those little gook mother-fuckers to fuck around with the First Air Cav.," the chopper door gunner yelled over his shoulder. But as we circled higher, out of the trajectory of the friendly incoming artillery rounds, one had the chilling realization that none of this was good news and could only mean that we had stumbled upon a hive of Viet Cong (VC) or North Vietnamese Army.

If I Die Before I Wake

When the shelling ceased, we broke the holding formation and again attempted our descent, but this time the pilot took no chances and dropped down into the valley that was the south side of the projected Landing Zone, away from the AK-47 and machine gun fire that we had encountered earlier. The rest of the Chinooks and the Infantry choppers followed, all spread out at a safe distance. As we came upon the south side of the hill, we hovered with our rotors spinning just below the hilltop where hopefully any remaining snipers or rockets would not find us. The pilot held his hover just long enough for us to say a quick prayer and jump to the steep clearing below that was now to become our new home, christened LZ Peanuts, as counterintuitive as it may seem by someone back at the Tactical Operations Center (TOC). The rest of the choppers wasted no time unloading the Infantry to quickly lift back, rolling off the hillside and returning down into the valley to safety before the VC had a chance to regroup after our Artillery shelling. The other six Chinooks, however, had more of an exposure and risk factor, as they had to come in high and hover to gently set down the Howitzers they had slung beneath onto the top of this finger of a knoll. Each Howitzer had to be placed one behind the next at equal distance to give each gun its needed space for its ammo dump and the men's bunkers. And then, these Chinooks still had to land and let the gun personnel out of the rear loading ramps. But, as it turned out, the rest of the afternoon was uneventful.

The FDC was always the first to land so we could achieve a temporary set-up, establish communication with our Colonel and Command Headquarters and get our guns 'on-line' ASAP. We stripped the jeep of the needed equipment and set up our map tables to get a quick fix on our location. Then, we worked up the basic data needed in case the enemy decided to welcome us with another attack. We didn't even take the time to dig in; our charts and maps were sitting on folding tables out in the open, right in front of God and the Devil. Our Howitzers were manually pulled and pushed into the proper position with fixed horizontal barrels – point blank, and loaded with 'Bee-hive' rounds which gave them the effect of a shotgun. The only real problem was with the LZ's steep sides, the shrapnel would most likely fire over the heads of any approaching enemy.

*   *   *

Following protocol, one platoon would stay behind to establish the LZ perimeter. This platoon quickly began digging in for their M-60 machine guns and guard bunkers, setting up trip flares and stringing out Claymore mines. By dusk, we were still sitting ducks but totally exhausted from the move and the constant draining 'fear factor' that Charley had left us with. Still, we pulled our appointed night shifts, slept hard when we could, and the next morning came too quickly with the basic business of constructing an LZ where once a mountaintop had been.

Shovels in hand, we first dug the FDC bunker; a four foot deep room-sized hole, approximately 12 feet square. The hard earth that was excavated from this hole we used to fill and pack sandbags, which were then stacked like walls staggered in a brick pattern around the perimeter of the bunker up to a ceiling roof height. We then placed steel runway tarmac over the top of the sandbags covering the bunker, and then continued stacking more and more sandbags over these steel roof sections that would become the only thing between us and the Grim Reaper. Next, we set up the antenna, the generator, checked the gas tank, and tied a 12-volt jeep headlight beneath the steel ceiling. This would soon become the only illumination in the LZ other than candles or flashlights. Finally, when all of this was accomplished, we cranked up the generator that would send its gas combustion noise echoing through the darkness to signal Charley we were now, officially 'open for business.' With the adequate glow from the ceiling headlight; we continued to set up and secure the topographic maps, the grid plotting tables, rolled out the phone lines to each of the six Howitzers and checked communication with the gun Sergeants. All the while, periodically checking with our Forward Observer (FO), who was already out in the jungle with the infantry platoons settling in for the evening. Finally, our basic Battery was up and running, ready to serve.

The next few days were quiet, too quiet. With all of the action and commotion associated with our landing, every Gook in Vietnam knew where we were. But why didn't they attack? At some point you just stopped asking and completed the construction of your personal hooch, much the same way as the FDC bunker but much smaller. It was hard work digging holes in virgin earth with only your shitty little entrenching tool, baking under the blazing jungle sun. Once the basic shell and roof were complete, I dragged a few empty ammo boxes from the gun's ammo dump, filled them with dirt, and stacked them up for a bed platform above the dirt floor; inflated my air mattress, placed it on top of this platform, hung my mosquito net, set out my pipe, pot, and hash at a convenient reachable distance from the bunk, pulled out my cassette tape player loaded with the latest Beatles cassettes – 'The Magical Mystery Tour,' and called it home.

*   *   *

At dusk, the mountains of this northern part of South Vietnam brought a false sense of serenity, throwing golden tones across the high streaming cirrus clouds and the majestic peaks that ran along the horizon of the Laotian border behind us. You could almost feel God's hand upon your shoulder. As the days continued with only basic fire missions being requested by our FO, the occasional flares, nothing serious, you found yourself quickly forgetting the welcoming party that Charley had waiting upon our first landing and found yourself wondering why this couldn't be the total experience of war. Why couldn't this be the worst of it? Smoke a daily pipe-load, watch the sunset, and fire a couple of fire missions, while away my year to become 'short' and go home. I couldn't wait to have those little squares on my helmet showing that I had only 99 days or less, 'left in country.' This was my wish, my dream, and it was settling in.

*　　　*　　　*

"You can kill ten of my men for every one I kill of yours. But even at those odds, you will lose, and I will win."

Ho Chi Minh words to a French visitor at the outset of their conflict, the French Indochina War of 1946 through 1954.

…Someone was shaking me. The cold Mountain Yard pipe swayed, still in its place, the bowl with the remnants of pot and hash nestled in the middle of my chest having waned cool and silent sometime in the middle of the night after the candles had long since flickered out. Did I sleep? Did I dream? Did I stare too long this time into the blue pearl eyes of the Dragon? In the mental haze of another morning I was having trouble pulling myself back, back from that dark abyss just below that edge where I had found peace, comfort, and escape; escape from everything except another twelve-hour shift in the FDC.

I pulled on my pants, boots, threw on a t-shirt and took a swig from my canteen to push myself up and my way out of the dark hooch, up into the bright morning light. My eyes squinting to finally focus on our little LZ jetting out with all six Howitzers evenly spaced, one following the other. Gun number six was positioned at the far end of the hill and number one was the closest, just down a small incline from our FDC. At the hilltop, adjacent to our Fire Direction Control bunker sat the dug-in infantry Tactical Operations Center. All of our personnel and the Officers had their personal hooches dug-in at this end of the mountaintop perimeter. On this particular morning our Landing Zone seemed to be floating within an ocean of white; where only two other distant island mountain peaks could be seen protruding through this thick creamy dense jungle fog as the sun shone lucent and warm reflecting above. I almost felt an inner peace standing there staring across this stunning horizon but that was only until the cool cloud-of-fog lifted to consume our LZ and once again bring the afternoon into a confused blurry haze. It was with this same afternoon haze that Charley really got his shit together and lobbed a mid-day mortar right at the feet of two of our infantry boys who just happened to be stepping out of their personal hooch at that exact moment . . . *'Death, up-close and personal.'*

You can't help but take a good-long look when it's your first. It's human instinct. "God, that could be me," everyone thought quietly passing in stunned procession. There really wasn't much left to see in that mortar crater where the entrance to their bunker had been only moments before. But you could smell it... Death. One thing was now obvious and present in everyone's mind, Charley finally had us bracketed and could hit us anytime he chose.

"Tell the Vietnamese they've got to draw in their horns or we're going to bomb them back into the Stone Age. ~"

President Lyndon B. Johnson

The Marines' 11th Engineers had begun moving down Route 9 deactivating mines and repairing bridges. They met with little to no resistance. The enemy shelling of Khe Sanh had become a matter of a few scattered rounds a day and it had been more than two weeks since General Westmoreland had revealed that, in his opinion, any other major attacks on Khe Sanh would never come. As we now know, he would later regret these words, believing the 304th NVA Division had left the area and so had the 325C. It seemed that all but a token force of the NVA had vanished.

Perhaps, as the United States claimed, the B-52's had driven them all away (We claimed 13,000 NVA dead from those raids). Maybe the majority of the North Vietnamese Army had left the Khe Sanh area as early as January 1968, leaving the Marines pinned down, to move across I Corps and down south to get ready for the next Tet Offensive.

Incredible arms caches were being found, rockets still crated, launchers still wrapped in factory paper, AK-47's still packed in military Cosmoline, all indicating that battalion-strength units had left in a hurry. Considering the amount of weapons and supplies being found (a record for the entire war), there were surprisingly few prisoners, although one prisoner did tell his interrogators that 75 percent of his regiment had been killed by our B-52's, nearly 1,500 men and that the survivors were starving. (The U.S. employed saturation-bombing techniques and delivered more than 110,000 tons of bombs to the hills surrounding Khe Sanh that General Westmoreland called Operation Pegasus) This was considered a victory, but the war was far from over.

Following Secretary of Defense Robert McNamara's Senate subcommittee testimony that "US bombing raids against North Vietnam had not achieved their objectives," around April 3, 1968, President Johnson restricted bombing in North Vietnam. Also feeling the pain of an unwinnable war, the President put a closing date on his own Administration.

*　　　*　　　*

"Now we have a problem in making our power credible, and Vietnam is the place."

John F. Kennedy, 1961

. . . I'm not sure what it is about the earth's atmosphere at sunset but every night Charley simply knew that our radio transmissions weren't worth a shit. All we could hear for sometimes up to an hour were broken words through static and squelch, and most times we lost contact altogether. We had to sit and wait. But not Charley, this is what he waited for. This is when his ghostly shadows would lurk through the thick jungles and hit our infantry units with an ambush and ensuing firefight. And by the time our Forward Observers were able to contact us and we were able to plot grid coordinates, determine what kind of fire mission was needed from the garbled cryptic confusion coming over our radio's small abused speaker, the battle could be over; our men could be butchered. This sunset was to be no exception. Charley had too much going for him to let this opportunity pass. The difference being, this time it was *our Battery* that was his objective of the day.

Just before dusk, they started shelling again, but this time not just the usual harassing mortar or two aimed anywhere in the vicinity of our LZ; this time it was an enthusiastic, continuous raining of mortars, with an occasional direct-fire rocket for good measure. What did they have to lose? This was not the time to ration their precious ammunition. They had us pinpointed. Ask those two dead infantry boys. They'll tell you it's true. They'll stand up, wave their dismembered arms and legs around in a 'wish-dance' - wishing they had never stepped out of that bunker. And sure enough, just before sunset, one of Charlie's direct-fire rockets hit the far end of our LZ and blew up our number 6 Howitzer's ammunition dump with a huge burst of fire and flame. This explosion was horrifying. We had no way to contain such a fire, not to mention we were still under a continuous downpour of enemy mortars. And now our pompous National Guard Officer, Captain Weiss, had a real challenge for his pseudo 'leadership capabilities.'

The Infantry commanding officers quickly descended the FDC bunker steps and ordered that all the perimeter Infantry, and our Howitzer boys were to pull back from the devastation and form a new perimeter between our Fire Direction Control bunker and the Infantry Tactical Operations Center. There, we would be safer from our own ammunition explosions. But this fire was jumping from gun to gun, working its way towards our FDC entrance. It was like we were being attacked, shelled by a 105 Howitzer battery with the random and devastating noise shaking the earth and compressing the air around us. At this point, all we could do was pray.

Dusk, paying no attention to the human dilemma held there within, quietly gave way to night. Someone fired up the generator to power the jeep headlight centered in the now overcrowded FDC. Infantry and Artillery personnel were jockeying for position under the safety of the sandbag and steel-reinforced ceiling. Most of the 'short-timers' were trying to work their way towards the rear of the hooch, away from the open entry with only a sandbag blast wall to protect it. We were all bracing ourselves for the inevitable.

I was stuck in the middle of this rigid gridlock of turmoil when someone popped a purple smoke marker and rolled it just outside of our bunker's entrance. This was quickly followed by the clamor and turbulence of a chopper sitting down in the tight incline between the number one Howitzer and our FDC. The dusty purple haze, mixed with sand and dirt, blew in swirls through the small slit of a window and the door opening to our sandbag sanctuary.

This whole scene was surreal. I tried to grasp what was happening, who, what, or why a Medevac team had been called and was now pushing their way down the dirt steps and through the crowded bunker. But all I could make out through the colored fog and eerie vagueness were helmeted silhouettes passing helmeted silhouettes.

The distant explosions of our own ammunition continued, with the now sporadic dropping of enemy mortars amongst the high pitched whining of the awaiting Medevac helicopter. Something was definitely happening. For our Captain and our leader, Ronald Weiss, the man who had requested Vietnam duty just to see 'what it would be like,' the man who wouldn't accept the National Guard as an answer to his military obligation, was now a bloated mass of collapsed responsibility. The Medevac team, not wanting to risk their lives or their chopper one moment longer than necessary, parted the congestion of excessive fear inside the bunker and carried our fallen commander on his olive drab canvas stretcher towards the bunker entry. Not one of the soldiers inside that crowded bunker wanted to be back up top. Not the short-timers, not the enlisted men, not the draftees, not the ranking officers, none of us. No one wanted the exposure to a most uncertain existence.

'Captain, oh my Captain', I thought sadly as this man turned his fat, sweaty head in my direction, glimpsing my eyes across that dark crowded bunker. As the Medevac team lifted his gurney up the bunker steps carrying the panicked betraying soul to the safety of the awaiting chopper, he mouthed the words with tears in his eyes, "I'm sorry." Then he was gone. This stopped me in my tracks. How could a 'professional,' a volunteer soldier be so weak as to allow himself the luxury of fear in the face of battle?

...The crowd within the FDC became unbearable. The

humidity mixed with the sweating dismay and stinking breath of dread was overwhelming. I, along with the other drafted men that really had no business in there (being that there was no way to do our job, conduct a Fire-Mission at this point, and we essentially no longer had an Artillery Battery), were ordered up top with the rest of the gun and infantry men by a ranking infantry officer that I did not recognize. All of us hesitated, but there was no way to honorably remain in the safety of that bunker. As I snapped up my Flak jacket, grabbed my M-16 with an extra satchel of ammo, I made my way up the dirt stairs of our defunct FDC, holding my helmet to my head; I just couldn't get the Captain's face out of my mind as he mouthed the words "I'm sorry."

Sometime just past dusk, Charley had stopped his incoming. But still, we had to manage through the long evening and night ahead, sitting on the bumpy sandbag roof of the FDC bunker, eating cold sea rations and waiting. Waiting...

*　　*　　*

Water was an issue and had already become scarce. We had no way to get to our water storage tank as our own ammo was still on fire with an occasional explosion sending hot shrapnel bursting through the thick air. So, we sat tight, rationed, and got as comfortable as possible lying on sandbags. The smoky haze had blown down wind and now the evening sky opened to a crystal clear map of the universe.

I found myself staring up at the millions of stars above and beyond, feeling, insignificant, adrift in an ocean of time. Somehow our entire LZ had become serene as our ammo exploding became more and more sporadic. A bizarre calmness fell over us, '*no doubt, the lull before the storm*,' I thought to myself. And though I wasn't a pessimist, a few of the guys were foolishly optimistic. "Let them come!" yelled one muscle bound angry scraper. Then, in his best John Wayne impersonation he spoke, "we'll-kill-those-little-Gook-mother-fuckers." The rest of us laid quietly, listening to the night, some prayed aloud to the God of their choice and all hoped against hope that maybe nothing would happen. Soon we were asleep . . .

. . . 0:315: A trip-flare went off at one of the remaining manned perimeter Guard Bunkers, as a half asleep infantryman grabbed and spun his .60 caliber machine gun to begin firing in panic as shadows darted and lurked in the perimeter before him. Seconds later, a couple of Claymore mines were set off from the next Guard Bunker, and then. . . chaos! Someone shot off a hand-flare and through the smoky yellow light I rolled off the top of the bunker as the rest of the men scattered, running anywhere, everywhere. I quickly crawled behind the small blast wall that protected the FDC entrance as the nightmare began. AK-47s and small caliber machine gun rounds were flying like a swarm of bees filling the air around us. From inside the FDC bunker, someone had already called for support and Cobra backup, but being so far North, it could take up to fifty minutes before we would see any relief; by then, we could all be dead. Our old abandoned position, where our six Howitzers now lay in helpless smoldering heaps of scrap-metal, was *crawling* with the enemy. We were surrounded and most certainly penetrated.

From this safer position where I squatted, with the shrill humming of AK-47 rounds puncturing the sandbags about me, I could only see occasional flashes, glimpses, more silhouettes darting across the backdrop of still burning ammunition boxes and rolling clouds of colored smoke highlighted by another hand-flare popping overhead by a 'heads-up' infantryman. As I huddled there, in that FDC doorway, viewing this collage of absurd confusion like some forbidden film, I realized that this was not the end, but the beginning. I was caught up in the moment that could only be described as the 'Birthplace of Death and all that was Evil.' It was here that I found my separateness and my union; for how could it be Evil to have that clarity of the moment.

An infantry officer had jumped up on top of the FDC bunker and was now screaming commands and waving directions overhead to anyone that would listen. *'Was he crying for attention, or possibly a 'war promotion?'* I wondered, as my ass puckered and I crouched lower still behind the blast wall. At least this infantry professional soldier didn't run away, he was into it.

"Hey guys, any room in there for me?" I yelled through the cacophony of exploding hand grenades, small arms, and machine gun fire into the FDC bunker just behind me. "No way man! We're full up" someone yelled from within. And they were. I knew that better than anyone. Still, there were more 'short timers' and chicken-shit First Lieutenants crammed into that FDC bunker than when I was ordered to leave. And for a brief second, I found myself wondering why? Weren't these officers trained for this shit? Weren't they supposed to lead, direct, and protect their men in battle? Why were so many of them huddled in the back of this bunker? Why was our Captain allowed to be Medevac'd out of the field with his 'self-proclaimed' Nervous Breakdown? Then, of course, the answer hit me and it was embarrassingly obvious and simple. "Death" . . . it was just that plain and unadorned. When it gets right down to it, down to the basic roots of survival, it is and always will be: "Every Man for Himself."

There are few enlightened souls who would give up his or her life for someone else. And with the nature of this unpopular war, it didn't breed many earnest heroes. No Audie Murphy's, no Jimmy Stuarts, no John Wayne types pulling the pin of a hand grenade with his teeth, casually sauntering through enemy lines to deliver death and take victory for himself and his country. This was most certainly not the movies; this was not the popular World War II. This was May 1968 and many of the youths knew that what we were doing was wrong. They were protesting this war on their college campuses. They were sliding flowers down the rifle barrels of the National Guard sent to keep the "Dirty-Commie-Hippies" under control and from rioting.

And even though this was before the "Fall of the Nixon Regime" and the 'Watergate Scandal,' this would be the last time any conscious American worth his constitutional rights would believe his or her government again without question; when they spewed forth the proclamation that, "The Communists Are Coming," or any other such propaganda. Meanwhile, I was halfway around the world questioning my own mortality, minute by minute, second by second, shallow breath by shallow breath. My skinny little twenty-year-old ass was stuck. Stuck in a moonless night and forced to fight for my life. And fight we did, squeezing off more rounds from my M-16 at darting shadows, dropping the ammo-clip out, flipping it over and slamming the next full clip into its locked position to firing again as the cries of the wounded laying somewhere out in the dark remains of our Landing Zone were now becoming pathetic vague whispers for 'help' or for 'death' to deliver them from the pain.

The infantry officer, still standing on the bunker above me took a hit to his shoulder and dropped to one knee. Grabbing the wound with his free hand he steadied himself, but almost as if nothing had happened, quickly stood back up and continued shouting directions, commanding men from his vantage point to different locations to protect and tighten our shrinking perimeter. I didn't know who this man was but he most certainly was a hero.

I, on the other hand, quickly began to low-crawl through the dirt around to the back of the FDC to try and make it to a perimeter foxhole for better protection. There, I might at least have a chance to put up some kind of honest fight before we were all killed. Two men dove into my place behind the FDC blast-wall and tried to bully and plunge their way into the FDC for safety. It was too crowded. They were probably as frightened as I was trying to cram down the dirt steps and into the refuge; but only hysteria and fighting broke out between our own men. Insanity.

Finally, a "Snoopy" Gun-Ship arrived dropping illumination flares that floated on small parachutes from above. When the flare canister popped, a shrill whistling followed the empty cartridge through the dark and to the earth below, leaving only its eerie yellow light. Through the smoky hue that cast elongated shadows across the battle-scarred site and wreckage that had been our solitary LZ only hours before, you could now witness an escalated killing frenzy of enemy on enemy on the battlefield below.

I had become frozen between the FDC bunker and the perimeter fox hole positions; crippled by some gripping chill that had captured me as I lay there in the dirt, shivering. *"Oh God in heaven . . . Save me!"* I found myself mumbling these words unconsciously in the fear and fermented uncertainty of war. *"Though I walk through the shadow of death . . . Please..."* I continued in a low whimper, my own breath blowing dust up into my face and eyes. I became too afraid to look up. Paralyzed as sickening odors filled my nostrils, for it now seemed that Death was by no means a shadow. It stood tall and brave; its angry presence encompassed me.

Strange, as next there came a lull in the fighting. This was the time for me to move. I got to my knees, quickly wiped the grime from my face, and did a low profile run to dive behind the now destroyed Infantry Tactical bunker. There I waited. Then I ran across the knoll and down the hillside, sliding into a perimeter foxhole with a couple of other lost souls challenged to recall their pledge of allegiance. There we fought, but also waited. . . waited to be among the crucified, those indifferently sacrificed on the altar of a country that no longer cared. For now, we knew how this night would surely end. And to what avail?

Another explosion erupted down by the remains of our artillery pieces sending more fire and billowing smoke from this bizarre stage. Two Cobra gun-ships arrived, dropping from the blackness above into the flare-lit night, hovering like giant black dragons above. They rotated, swirled, and spun in a controlled maneuver, spotting the multiple infiltrators; they lifted their tails and fired rockets into the onslaught of gooks that were still crawling through the perimeter wire and up the hillside. The red tracers of their Miniguns looked like a waving blood-vein of light as they sprayed around the enemy intrusion below. But the truth was, we were overrun and the little fuckers were everywhere.

The Cobras couldn't do the job they wanted without killing their own. I started firing my M-16 again, randomly, at any movement in the perimeter darkness below or in the direction of the Howitzer graveyard of twisted metal and fiery explosions. I mowed the general vicinity, changed ammo clips when empty and mowed again. The apparitions were running amok while death danced to the beat of the explosions and the cries of the dying. I no longer knew who was who but became crazed, possessed to keep firing as Death's face swayed enticingly before me; her tongue flapping as the exotic stench of sulfur and burning flesh filled my head and took its slow sweet time to descend to the depths of my soul. There, she impregnated me with her seed of decay and disgust for all that was moral and humane therein. And, if I listened carefully, I could hear her summons with just the faintest of whispers, "Where-is-your-God-now? . . . Where-is-your-God-now?"

*   *   *

"Let us understand: North Vietnam cannot defeat or humiliate the United States. Only Americans can do that."

President Richard M. Nixon, 1969

By sunrise, what was left of the VC had retreated, disappeared back into the dawn. After what had seemed like countless incarnations of fighting, hiding, blind crawling through the earth and debris to scramble and fight again, all of which had occurred within that one early morning of pure uncultivated Hell, this 'new dawn' was breathing a renewed sense of reality and hope. But we were all too tired, too thirsty, too hungry, and no doubt in shock to even realize, as the warmth of the morning sun hit the remains of LZ Peanuts, that we were in fact the lucky ones. We had made it when many of our Battery and our supporting Infantry Platoon hadn't. The guys you had lived with, ate with, laughed with; the guys that you shared thoughts and plans with, were now lying dead, torn bodies scattered around the remains and dismay of this twisted LZ graveyard.

But all of these young men, and more, including the infantrymen I did not know, now had been transformed into heavy dead weight in blood-filled olive drab ponchos. I sweated and strained that entire morning, lifting and dragging their lifeless remains to the designated 'pick-up' point above our smoldering battle torn hillside. This was the first and only time I betrayed my father's 'advice' and volunteered for this duty. Morbid curiosity? Experience? I'm not sure which, but my mind couldn't help but race to their families and loved ones; the proud mothers and fathers who were all, perhaps *at that very moment*, writing letters, making plans, baking the goodies for the next 'care-package' to be sent to Vietnam to their sons. They had no way of knowing.

Would they, these patriotic parents, torture themselves afterward, after they found out just how pathetic our government was with its lies? After they found out how utterly useless this war truly was? Probably not, a loss of this magnitude cuts into the heart, forever to remain a hard memory you had to learn to live with.

After my farewell to these friends and the brave Infantry and Gun Personnel that I had helped place for pick-up, I was brought back to the realization of where I was, and the long wait before evacuation, by the intense screaming of a Vietnamese just beyond a destroyed infantry bunker. I walked over to take a look, anything to take my mind off of my desperate thirst and the remains I had just left on the awaiting hillside. I climbed over disheveled sandbags and up onto the top of that bunker to find an Arvin Ranger. This Vietnamese soldier had signed up and was trained by the U.S. to fight and translate, but he was now slapping a captured NVA soldier with a closed fist, spitting piercing questions into his young, soot-smeared camouflaged face. The young enemy, placed on his knees with his hands bound tightly behind his back, bloodied with communication wire, would not speak. He was an ancient warrior. Dressed in nothing but a filthy loincloth. Barefoot he carried a satchel for his tools of death and destruction. Still, he was proud. You could see it in his face, in his body language, shoulders back, head held high. He looked straight into the soul of the Arvin's eyes with disdain. It was an inbred trait; the people of Vietnam had spent too many years in conflict to talk to the likes of this Arvin traitor. But without a second chance or warning, in one fluid motion, the Ranger popped a quick shot to the left side of the Gook's head with an ivory-handled Colt 45 revolver. The entire right side of this young soldier's head exploded as he collapsed, falling over the two other dead prisoners that had held their tongues before him. The truth was, both of the other two Gooks did talk; we (the U.S. of A.) just didn't want the hassle or the paperwork of dragging their stinking asses back to Base Camp for processing.

I walked back over the hillside to where the survivors of our artillery personnel were sitting, scattered amongst the last of the Infantrymen, all waiting patiently for our evacuation from Armageddon. I had to beg for some water from one of these men, as I could no longer go without. He didn't have any extra to spare, but he didn't say that, passing me his canteen. We sat together in silence, and waited.

Eventually, much later that afternoon, the Chinooks and Hueys finally did arrive. They picked up our remains from that little finger of a knoll and lifted us to safety without a single shot being fired from our enemy. The flight back across that mountain range, the jungles and rolling hills below was a solemn one. Even the Gung-ho infantry boys with their Gook-ear-necklaces, who drank beer from the skulls of their dead enemy, sat in quiet reverence for the battle not lost, but certainly not won. We all stared, disoriented, across the war-raped landscape to the pastel colored clouds drifting on the horizon, turning to a golden violet as the earth slowly rotated – revolving to a dusky twilight; perhaps God did answer my prayers.

© g.h. cline

Edited by Blue Mount Publishing - with Special Thanks to Windsor Betts for her meticulous skills and to Christophe Adajar & Ed Salven.

*"**NOT EVERYONE WHO LOST HIS LIFE IN VIETNAM DIED THERE, NOT EVERYONE WHO CAME HOME FROM VIETNAM EVER LEFT THERE.**"*

Anonymous

LZ PEANUTS BEFORE

LZ PEANUTS AFTER

About The Author

G. H. CLINE

G. H. Cline wrote original songs and played in a popular 'Garage Rock' Band throughout Hollywood's Sunset Strip in the mid-1960s. Drafted in 1967, he spent all of 1968 in combat in Vietnam.

Upon his return, he continued in the Rock 'n' Roll scene, now writing poetry and continuing with original music. He started his own Custom Home Construction Company in the 1970s while continuing his creative endeavors. His two poetry books, 'Consider The Source (2006) and 'Treading Eclectic Waters' (2007), along with a much overdue Vietnam short story about his combat experience; 'If I Die Before I Wake' (2012), were all well received by his close friends and peers. Now retired from the construction business, he has focused on his creativity, and publishing his short stories.